The Story of America

THE AMERICAN REVOLUTION

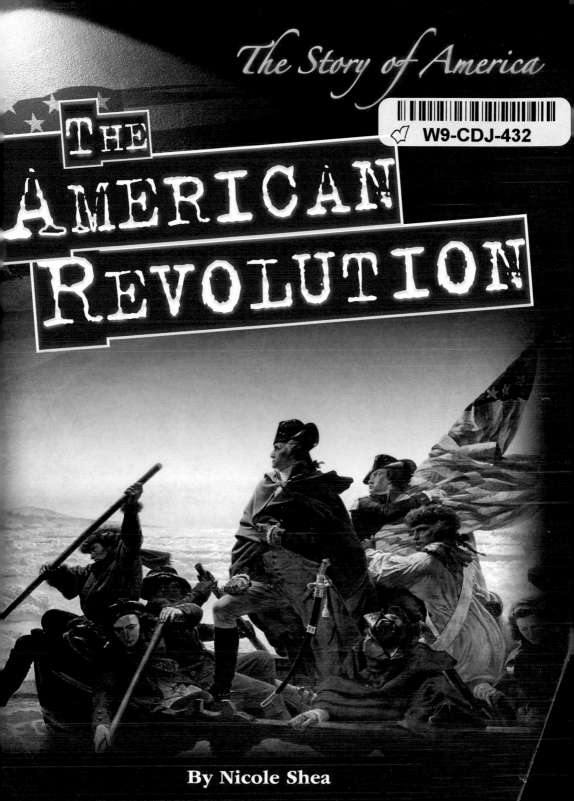

By Nicole Shea

Gareth Stevens
Publishing

Please visit our Web site, www.garethstevens.com. For a free color catalog of all our high-quality books, call toll free 1-800-542-2595 or fax 1-877-542-2596.

Library of Congress Cataloging-in-Publication Data

Shea, Nicole.
 The American Revolution / Nicole Shea.
     p. cm. — (Story of America)
 Includes index.
 ISBN 978-1-4339-4761-2 (pbk.)
 ISBN 978-1-4339-4762-9 (6-pack)
 ISBN 978-1-4339-4760-5 (library binding)
 1. United States—History—Revolution, 1775-1783—Juvenile literature. I. Title.
 E208.S47 2011
 973.3–dc22

                                        2010035556

First Edition

Published in 2011 by
Gareth Stevens Publishing
111 East 14th Street, Suite 349
New York, NY 10003

Copyright © 2011 Gareth Stevens Publishing

Designer: Daniel Hosek
Editor: Therese Shea

Photo credits: Cover, pp. 1, 17, 20–21 Popperfoto/Getty Images; pp. 4, 14, 19 (main image) Stock Montage/Getty Images; pp. 5, 6, 11, 15 (*Common Sense*), 23, 24 MPI/Getty Images; pp. 7, 12–13, 15 (Paine), 25, 27 (Lafayette), 29 Hulton Archive/Getty Images; p. 8 English School/The Bridgeman Art Library/Getty Images; p. 9 Fotosearch/Getty Images; p. 19 (Hancock signature) Shutterstock.com; p. 22 Superstock/Getty Images; p. 27 (surrender of Cornwallis) Marie Hansen/Time & Life Pictures/Getty Images.

Printed in the United States of America

CPSIA compliance information: Batch #CR118221GS: For further information contact Gareth Stevens, New York, New York at 1-800-542-2595.

Contents

Words in the glossary appear in **bold** type the first time they are used in the

The Beginning

How was it possible that fewer than 3 million American colonists took on the entire British Empire? John Adams said, "The Revolution was effected before the War **commenced**. The Revolution was in the heart and minds of the people." Like Adams, some people argue that the American Revolution—also known as the Revolutionary War—started much earlier than 1775, when the first shots were fired. Years before, the hearts and minds of the colonists had turned against British rule.

A poor British economy in the 1760s and 1770s contributed to the start of the revolution. England had spent a lot of money fighting wars and was in financial trouble. The British were looking for ways to raise money. They soon looked to their thirteen colonies in North America.

John Adams ▷

DID YOU KNOW?

John Adams was an early supporter of American independence who lived in Massachusetts. He was one of the Founding Fathers of the United States and later a U.S. president.

Both the French and British had Native American allies in the French and Indian War.

The Seven Years' War

The Seven Years' War (1756–1763) was fought in Europe, North America, and India. The colonial rivalry between France and Britain over North America and India was a key cause of the war. Conflicts between these nations within the United States came to be called the French and Indian War. Future U.S. president George Washington fought in several battles for the British, rising to the rank of brigadier general. He had two horses shot from beneath him!

Boycotting the British

The British government imposed new taxes on its thirteen colonies under the **Revenue** Act of 1764. The colonists called it the Sugar Act because every time they bought sugar and molasses from the British, they were taxed. In March 1765, the British issued the Stamp Act, taxing legal documents, newspapers, and even playing cards.

THE FOLLY OF ENGLAND AND THE RUIN OF AMERICA

This drawing shows an angry mob in New York protesting the Stamp Act of 1765.

The British needed the money to help pay for their army in the colonies. That same year, England issued the Quartering Act, which required colonists to house and feed British troops. Without representatives in the British **Parliament**, colonists had no say in new laws and taxes. When England introduced the Townshend Acts in 1767—taxing paint, paper, and tea—the colonists began to act. Many decided to **boycott** certain British products.

The Townshend Acts

The Townshend Acts are named after Charles Townshend, who was the head of the British Treasury. The taxes were meant to pay the salaries of judges and governors in the colonies. Originally, the colonial governments had paid for these salaries. With the Townshend Acts, England had full control over the salaries, so the colonists couldn't punish the actions of British officials by reducing or withholding their salaries.

◄ Charles Townshend

DID YOU KNOW?

The Sugar Act was passed years after the Molasses Act of 1733. This previous act had never seriously been enforced.

The Patriots Protest

Colonists labeling themselves "patriots" were ready to fight the British laws. The anger towards the Stamp Act was so great that the British decided to abolish it. However, patriots were still eager to **rebel** against British control and other hated tax acts.

Though shown here in daylight, the Boston Tea Party took place at night so that no one was caught.

Riots broke out when England announced a complete monopoly on tea in the colonies. On April 1, 1774, patriots called the Sons of Liberty dressed as Native Americans and dumped 342 cases of British tea into Boston Harbor. The British punished the colonists by passing more laws in 1774. The Coercive Acts ordered the harbor closed until the colonists paid for the damage caused by the "Boston Tea Party." Because the colonists felt the Coercive Acts ignored their rights as British citizens, they renamed the laws the Intolerable Acts.

The Boston Massacre

In 1770, a riot broke out when colonists began to throw sticks, snowballs, and stones at a British soldier. When additional British soldiers were called for help, they were attacked, too. The soldiers then fired into the mob, killing five people. This incident became known as the Boston Massacre. John Adams, a future president of the United States, was the lawyer for the British soldiers accused of murder. Although Adams disliked the British presence in Boston, he wanted to be sure there was a fair trial.

A particular Account of the most barbarous and
HORRID MASSACRE!
Committed in King-Street, Boston, on Monday, March 5, 1770. by the Soldiers quartered in said Town.

DID YOU KNOW?

The tea ruined by the colonists would be worth more than $1 million today.

Lexington and Concord

The patriots were ready to fight. They collected weapons and other supplies. Some of these were stored in the town of Concord, Massachusetts. British soldiers—also called Redcoats for their uniform color—received orders to take away or destroy these weapons.

On the night of April 18, 1775, Paul Revere—a patriot and messenger—was told to warn the people of Concord of the Redcoats' approach. He was also to warn Samuel Adams and John Hancock of British orders for their arrest. A signal was arranged. The pastor of North Church would shine one light from the church tower if the British came by land and two if they approached by sea. That night, two lights were seen. Revere spread the news on horseback.

DID YOU KNOW?

Paul Revere was not the only rider the night of April 18, 1775. William Dawes and Samuel Prescott helped spread the word. Dawes and Revere were captured, but Prescott escaped to Concord.

The First Continental Congress

On September 5, 1774, a group of colonial representatives gathered in Philadelphia. Each colony except Georgia sent several delegates to what was called the First Continental Congress. The Congress declared that only colonial governments should be able to tax the colonists. They agreed to a boycott of all British products. They demanded that all British colonial taxes be abolished and that the British army be removed. They also asked the British king, George III, for help.

Paul Revere (shown here on horseback) borrowed a horse for his famous ride. It was later taken by the British.

By the time British troops reached the town of Lexington on April 19, 1775, they faced about 77 patriots from the Massachusetts **militia**, ready to fight. The militia members received the name "minutemen" because they were expected to be ready for battle at a minute's notice. Though quick to respond, the minutemen were too few against a British force of about 700.

The British troops marched on to Concord, where they searched for weapons. When the British

This illustration of the conflict at Lexington shows the orderly British troops parading by the hastily assembled American militia.

began their march back to Boston, they were met by more minutemen. Even farmers joined in the fight. In the end, 273 British and 95 colonists were killed. The bloodshed caused many more Americans to become patriots. More militias formed in other colonies. The American Revolution had begun.

A Promise of Freedom

The British tried forming partnerships with slaves in the colonies in order to increase the size of their army. In November 1775, they promised freedom to any slave who fought on their side. As a result, many slaves escaped and supported the British as a way of gaining freedom. In fact, 300 slaves joined the British army within a month of the announcement.

DID YOU KNOW?

No one knows who fired the first shots of the American Revolution.

Washington's Army

On May 10, 1775, the Second Continental Congress met in Philadelphia. Within this assembly were famous patriots, such as Samuel Adams, John Adams, John Hancock, Patrick Henry, Benjamin Franklin, and Thomas Jefferson. This Congress turned the Boston militia into the main force of their Continental army. They made George Washington commander in chief of this army.

Washington was perfect for the position because of his accomplishments in the French and Indian War, and also because he was from Virginia. Many in the South opposed the war. The Congress hoped the respected Washington could gather southern support.

Before the American Revolution, George Washington was a longtime member of the Virginia colonial government.

Common Sense

Thomas Paine was a patriot from England who moved to Pennsylvania in 1774 hoping for a new life. In January 1776, Paine published a booklet called *Common Sense*. In it, Paine challenged the idea of a king who held power over his people. He argued that people should rule themselves. This principle of **democracy** became a cornerstone of the United States. More than 100,000 copies of *Common Sense* were sold.

Thomas Paine

The Congress also issued new paper money. They borrowed money from countries overseas in order to pay soldiers and buy military supplies. Money was a constant problem throughout the American Revolution.

DID YOU KNOW?

The Second Continental Congress sent a list of complaints and requests to King George III called the Olive Branch **Petition**. In return, the king sent 20,000 more troops to the colonies.

Battle on the Hill

On June 17, 1775, the inexperienced Continental army met British forces at Breed's Hill. This location, across from Boston, was an important site for control of the city. The Americans held their ground well. In the end, they ran out of **ammunition** and resorted to firing nails and glass at the Redcoats. Even though the Americans had to retreat, they had surprised the enemy, who had expected the army to fall quickly. The British had won the battle, but they had lost hundreds more soldiers than the colonists.

In March 1776, a victory for Washington's army at Dorchester Heights forced the British from Boston and the colonies, and into Canada. They would be back, but it was obvious that they wouldn't win easily.

DID YOU KNOW?

Despite the fact that the battle took place mainly on and around Breed's Hill, it's known as the Battle of Bunker Hill. Bunker Hill was next to Breed's Hill.

This image of the Battle of Bunker Hill shows the Americans defending their position while smoke from cannons swirls around them.

Famous Words at Bunker Hill

The Battle of Bunker Hill was the origin of the famous phrase: "Don't fire until you see the whites of their eyes." This order was important since the American soldiers didn't have much ammunition. They didn't want to waste what they did have on enemy soldiers who were too far away. No one is sure which American officer said it.

The Declaration of Independence

After 2 years of bloodshed and battles, a peaceful solution to the conflict between the colonies and England seemed impossible. By June 1776, the Second Continental Congress decided to break away from England once and for all. The Continental Congress assigned five representatives to write a document outlining reasons why the colonies were separating from England. The committee included Benjamin Franklin, John Adams, Roger Sherman, Robert Livingston, and Thomas Jefferson.

Mostly penned by Jefferson, the Declaration of Independence stated that the rights of citizens were more essential than a government's power. It said an unjust government must be overthrown if certain rights were threatened. Among those rights were "life, liberty, and the pursuit of happiness." The document was signed by 56 representatives of the "united states of America."

DID YOU KNOW?

Independence Day, or the Fourth of July, celebrates the day the Congress approved the wording of the Declaration of Independence.

The members of the "Declaration Committee" discuss the famous document. Benjamin Franklin is shown at left, while Thomas Jefferson holds the Declaration of Independence.

John Hancock

John Hancock became president of the Second Continental Congress in 1776. It's said that Hancock wanted to make sure King George III could read his name on the Declaration of Independence without his reading glasses, so Hancock signed his name in large, bold letters. To this day, people sometimes refer to a signature as a "John Hancock."

A Christmas Victory

Washington's rival at Dorchester Heights—General William Howe—landed in New York in July 1776 with 32,000 troops. At the Battle of Long Island, about 20,000 of these soldiers forced Washington's army into New York City. Washington and his men were then driven into New Jersey, giving up New York City. Pushed again—this time into Pennsylvania—the Continental army's spirits were low. However, Washington had a plan.

Despite raging winds and icy currents, George Washington is pictured standing tall and determined as American soldiers cross the Delaware River.

On the snowy night of December 25, 1776, the Continental army crossed the Delaware River into New Jersey. Washington knew that British allies, German **mercenary** soldiers called Hessians, were camped near Trenton. The Americans surprised and captured more than 900 Hessians and didn't lose a single American life. Washington's forces moved further into New Jersey, capturing Princeton. These victories boosted American spirits.

Women in War

The American Revolution wasn't just a man's war. Many women contributed to America's fight for independence. Some mended soldiers' uniforms. Others accompanied troops as nurses, taking care of wounded and dying soldiers. Many women worked as cooks. Women weren't allowed to be soldiers back then. However, there are several records of women dressing up as men in order to fight.

DID YOU KNOW?

As the fighting grew closer, the Continental Congress moved from Philadelphia, Pennsylvania, to Baltimore, Maryland.

Turning Points

In 1777, two battles near Philadelphia—at Brandywine Creek and Germantown—ended in American defeats. However, American forces stopped British general John Burgoyne's forces from marching across New York. Burgoyne surrendered 5,700 soldiers on October 17, 1777. The Battle of Saratoga is considered to be the turning point of the revolution. It convinced France that the United States could win. France promised to send aid and soldiers.

The misery of the winter at Valley Forge is shown on the faces in this painting. Washington salutes his soldiers' bravery.

While waiting for the promised aid, the Continental army underwent extreme hardship during the winter of 1777–1778. Washington's men camped at Valley Forge in Pennsylvania. Illness, lack of food and clothes, and freezing weather caused thousands to leave the army. However, those who didn't leave became better soldiers. Washington asked a skilled German soldier named Friedrich von Steuben to teach the soldiers better ways to fight on the battlefield.

DID YOU KNOW?

Although Friedrich von Steuben is sometimes labeled a general or baron, he was neither! He was, however, a very skilled soldier.

Benedict Arnold, Patriot or Loyalist?

About one-fifth of American colonists were Loyalists, or people who were loyal to England during the American Revolution. One well-known Loyalist is Benedict Arnold. He wasn't always a Loyalist, though. Arnold was a successful American general who had an important role in the American victory at Saratoga. He later switched sides and became a spy for the British. Nearly hanged for betraying the Americans, he escaped and eventually moved to England.

◄ Benedict Arnold

On June 28, 1778, the Continental army fought its last major battle in the north at the Battle of Monmouth in New Jersey. There was no clear victor. However, Britain began to focus its war efforts in the South where many Loyalists lived. In December 1778, the Americans lost Savannah, Georgia. In 1780, the Redcoats took the cities of Charleston and Camden in South Carolina, too.

American forces (left) are shown on the attack at the Battle of Cowpens in South Carolina.

American general Nathanael Greene took command of the southern Continental army. He led his men, and many militia forces, against the British forces of General Charles Cornwallis. Americans were the victors in the battles of Kings Mountain and Cowpens in South Carolina, followed by another at Guilford Courthouse in North Carolina. Cornwallis and his forces fled to the Atlantic coast and up into Virginia.

DID YOU KNOW?

Several rebel groups in the South surprised the British. Francis Marion, known as the "Swamp Fox," used his knowledge of the swamps to launch surprise attacks on the British then disappear to safety in the swamps.

Molly Pitcher

The Battle of Monmouth is remembered for the story of Molly Pitcher. Her real name was Mary Hays McCauley, or Mary Hays. She accompanied her husband, who was in the Continental army. According to legend, Mary carried pitchers of water to cool the battlefield cannons. That's how she got her nickname. Soldiers called out for her: "Molly, pitcher!" Some even say that when Mary's husband fell ill or was wounded, she took his place at a cannon.

Mary Hays

Final Victories

By mid-1781, General Cornwallis had taken his British forces to the port of Yorktown in Virginia. The Marquis (mahr-KEE) de Lafayette, a French general, kept watch close by. Washington and French general Rochambeau made a plan. While making the British believe the Continental army was going to attack New York City, they moved 16,000 soldiers south. The Americans surrounded Yorktown. Cornwallis couldn't get help by way of the Chesapeake Bay, thanks to the French navy. His army was vastly outnumbered with no hope of relief.

On October 19, Cornwallis surrendered, ending the last battle of the Revolutionary War. The British still controlled several major American cities. However, the war had become unpopular in England, and Parliament agreed to end the conflict.

DID YOU KNOW?

Marie Joseph Paul Yves Roch Gilbert du Motier—the Marquis de Lafayette—bought his own ship to sail to America to help the Continental army. He played a major part in the French lending aid to the Americans.

Though shown in this painting surrendering to George Washington, Charles Cornwallis didn't actually take part in the official ceremony.

The Surrender

British general Charles Cornwallis didn't take part in the surrender ceremony with George Washington, claiming that he was ill. Instead, he sent his second in command, Brigadier General Charles O'Hara. A British band played the song "The World Turned Upside Down." General Lafayette then asked the band to play "Yankee Doodle."

the Marquis de Lafayette ▶

The Treaty of Paris

On September 3, 1783, the American Revolution officially ended with the signing of the Treaty of Paris. As representatives of the United States, Benjamin Franklin, John Adams, and John Jay signed the treaty. In the document, England formally recognized the United States as an independent country. The treaty also named the Mississippi River as the new nation's western boundary.

The new United States of America was free. Now the task before the Americans was to create a nation that honored the ideals and rights for which they had fought.

Timeline

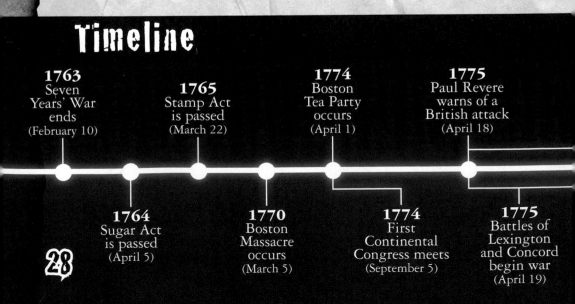

1763 Seven Years' War ends (February 10)

1764 Sugar Act is passed (April 5)

1765 Stamp Act is passed (March 22)

1770 Boston Massacre occurs (March 5)

1774 Boston Tea Party occurs (April 1)

1774 First Continental Congress meets (September 5)

1775 Paul Revere warns of a British attack (April 18)

1775 Battles of Lexington and Concord begin war (April 19)

D Hartley

David Hartley (top signature) was the British official who signed the Treaty of Paris in 1783.

John Adams

Franklin

John Jay

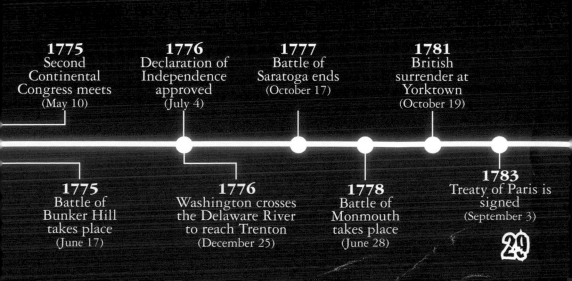

1775
Second
Continental
Congress meets
(May 10)

1776
Declaration of
Independence
approved
(July 4)

1777
Battle of
Saratoga ends
(October 17)

1781
British
surrender at
Yorktown
(October 19)

1775
Battle of
Bunker Hill
takes place
(June 17)

1776
Washington crosses
the Delaware River
to reach Trenton
(December 25)

1778
Battle of
Monmouth
takes place
(June 28)

1783
Treaty of Paris is
signed
(September 3)

Glossary

ammunition: bullets, shells, and other objects used as weapons

boycott: to refuse to buy or use products in protest against a group

coercive: using force to make people do things against their will

commence: to begin

democracy: government in which the people hold supreme power and choose their leaders

intolerable: so bad, difficult, or painful that it cannot be endured

massacre: the cruel killing of a large number of people

mercenary: a soldier hired to fight for another country

militia: a military force composed of citizens, used in emergencies

monopoly: a situation in which only one company controls an industry or product

Parliament: the lawmaking body of England

petition: a written request signed by many people asking the government to take an action

rebel: to fight to overthrow a government. Also, one who fights to overthrow it.

revenue: money that comes from the sale of goods or services

riot: a public disturbance during which a group of angry people become noisy and out of control

For More Information

BOOKS

Espinosa, Rod. *American Revolution*. Edina, MN: Magic Wagon, 2009.

Schanzer, Rosalyn. *George vs. George: The American Revolution As Seen from Both Sides*. Washington, DC: National Geographic, 2004.

Strum, Richard M. *Causes of the American Revolution*. Stockton, NJ: OTTN Publishing, 2006.

WEB SITES

The American Revolution: Lighting Freedom's Flame
www.nps.gov/revwar
Learn about the American Revolution, including stories, timelines, and links to much more.

Liberty! The American Revolution
www.pbs.org/ktca/liberty/chronicle.html
Read about the major events of the American Revolution in newspaper format.

Index